STUDY OF ENGLISH GRAMMAR-I

ESSAY WRITING

KABIR DAS

ISBN 979-888546103-0

Contents

I
General Essay Writing Tips

General Essay Writing Tips

Despite the fact that, as Shakespeare said, "the pen is mightier than the sword," the pen itself is not enough to make an effective writer. In fact, though we may all like to think of ourselves as the next Shakespeare, inspiration alone is not the key to effective essay writing. You see, the conventions of English essays are more formulaic than you might think – and, in many ways, it can be as simple as counting to five.

Steps to Writing an Essay

Follow these 7 steps for the best results:

1. **Read and understand the prompt**: Know exactly what is being asked of you. It's a good idea to dissect the prompt into parts.

2. **Plan**: Brainstorming and organizing your ideas will make your life much easier when you go to write your essay. It's a good idea to make a web of your ideas and supporting details.

3. **Use and cite sources**: Do your research. Use quotes and paraphrase from your sources, but NEVER plagiarize.

4. **Write a Draft**: Ernest Hemingway once said, "The first draft of anything is always crap." While the truth behind this statement

is debatable, drafts are always a good place to get any of your "crappy" ideas out of the way and are often required by professors and instructors.

5. **Make a strong thesis:** The thesis (main argument) of the essay is the most important thing you'll write. Make it a strong point.

6. **Respond to the prompt:** Once you have worked out any kinks in your draft, you can start writing the final draft of your essay.

7. **Proofread:** Read your response carefully to make sure that there are no mistakes and that you didn't miss anything.

Of course, every essay assignment is different and it's important to be mindful of that. If one of these steps isn't applicable to the essay you are writing, skip it and move to the next one.

The Five Paragraph Essay

Though more advanced academic papers are a category all their own, the basic high school or college essay has the following standardized, five paragraph structure:

- Paragraph 1: Introduction
- Paragraph 2: Body 1
- Paragraph 3: Body 2
- Paragraph 4: Body 3
- Paragraph 5: Conclusion

Though it may seem formulaic – and, well, it is - the idea behind this structure is to make it easier for the reader to navigate the ideas put forth in an essay. You see, if your essay has the same structure as every other one, any reader should be able to quickly and easily find the information most relevant to them.

The Introduction

Want to see sample essays?

Check out our Sample from second chepter where you can see scholarship essays, admissions essays, and more!

The principle purpose of the introduction is to present your position (this is also known as the "thesis" or "argument") on the issue at hand but effective introductory paragraphs are so much more than that. Before you even get to this thesis statement, for example, the essay should begin with a "hook" that grabs the reader's attention and makes them want to read on. Examples of effective hooks include relevant quotations ("no man is an island") or surprising statistics ("three out of four doctors report that...").

Only then, with the reader's attention "hooked," should you move on to the thesis. The thesis should be a clear, one-sentence explanation of your position that leaves no doubt in the reader's mind about which side you are on from the beginning of your essay.

Following the thesis, you should provide a mini-outline which previews the examples you will use to support your thesis in the rest of the essay. Not only does this tell the reader what to expect in the paragraphs to come but it also gives them a clearer understanding of what the essay is about.

Finally, designing the last sentence in this way has the added benefit of seamlessly moving the reader to the first paragraph of the body of the paper. In this way we can see that the basic introduction does not need to be much more than three or four sentences in length. If yours is much longer you might want to consider editing it down a bit!

Here, by way of example, is an introductory paragraph to an essay in response to the following question:

"Do we learn more from finding out that we have made mistakes or from our successful actions?"

"No man is an island" and, as such, he is constantly shaped and influenced by his experiences. People learn by doing and, accordingly, learn considerably more from their mistakes than their success. For proof of this, consider examples from both science and everyday experience.

The Body Paragraphs

The middle paragraphs of the essay are collectively known as the body paragraphs and, as alluded to above, the main purpose of a body paragraph is to spell out in detail the examples that support your thesis.

For the first body paragraph you should use your strongest argument or most significant example unless some other more obvious beginning point (as in the case of chronological explanations) is required. The first sentence of this paragraph should be the topic sentence of the paragraph that directly relates to the examples listed in the mini-outline of introductory paragraph.

A one sentence body paragraph that simply cites the example of "George Washington" or "LeBron James" is not enough, however. No, following this an effective essay will follow up on this topic sentence by explaining to the reader, in detail, who or what an example is and, more importantly, why that example is relevant.

Even the most famous examples need context. For example, George Washington's life was extremely complex – by using him as an example, do you intend to refer to his honesty, bravery, or maybe even his wooden teeth? The reader needs to know this and it is your job as the writer to paint the appropriate picture for them. To do this, it is a good idea to provide the reader with five or six relevant facts about the life (in general) or event (in particular) you believe most clearly illustrates your point.

Having done that, you then need to explain exactly why this example proves your thesis. The importance of this step cannot be understated (although it clearly can be underlined); this is, after all, the whole reason you are providing the example in the first place. **Seal the deal by directly stating why this example is relevant.**

Here is an example of a body paragraph to continue the essay begun above:

Take, by way of example, Thomas Edison. The famed American inventor rose to prominence in the late 19th century because of his successes, yes, but even he felt that these successes were the result of his many failures. He did not succeed in his work on one of his most famous inventions, the lightbulb, on his first try nor even on his hundred and first try. In fact, it took him more than 1,000 attempts to make the first incandescent bulb but, along the way, he learned quite a deal. As he himself said, "I did not fail a thousand times but instead succeeded in finding a thousand ways it would not work." Thus Edison demonstrated both in thought and action how instructive mistakes can be.

A Word on Transitions

You may have noticed that, though the above paragraph aligns pretty closely with the provided outline, there is one large exception: the first few words. These words are example of a transitional phrase – others include "furthermore," "moreover," but also "by contrast" and "on the other hand" – and are the hallmark of good writing.

Transitional phrases are useful for showing the reader where one section ends and another begins. It may be helpful to see them as the written equivalent of the kinds of spoken cues used in formal speeches that signal the end of one set of ideas and the beginning of another. In essence, they lead the reader from one section of the paragraph of another.

To further illustrate this, consider the second body paragraph of our example essay:

In a similar way, we are all like Edison in our own way. Whenever we learn a new skill - be it riding a bike, driving a car, or cooking a cake - we learn from our mistakes. Few, if any, are ready to go from training wheels to a marathon in a single day but these early experiences (these so-called mistakes) can help us improve our performance over time. You cannot make a cake without breaking a few eggs and, likewise, we learn by doing and doing inevitably means making mistakes.

Hopefully this example not only provides another example of an effective body paragraph but also illustrates how transitional phrases can be used to distinguish between them.

The Conclusion

Although the conclusion paragraph comes at the end of your essay it should not be seen as an afterthought. As the final paragraph is represents your last chance to make your case and, as such, should follow an extremely rigid format.

One way to think of the conclusion is, paradoxically, as a second introduction because it does in fact contain many of the same features. While it does not need to be too long – four well-crafted sentence should be enough – it can make or break and essay.

Effective conclusions open with a concluding transition ("in conclusion," "in the end," etc.) and an allusion to the "hook" used in the introductory paragraph. After that you should immediately provide a restatement of your thesis statement.

This should be the fourth or fifth time you have repeated your thesis so while you should use a variety of word choice in the body paragraphs it is a acceptable idea to use some (but not all) of the original language you used in the introduction. This echoing effect not only reinforces your argument but also ties it nicely to the second key element of the conclusion: a brief (two or three words is enough) review of the three main points from the body of the paper.

Having done all of that, the final element – and final sentence in your essay – should be a "global statement" or "call to action" that gives the reader signals that the discussion has come to an end.

In the end, then, one thing is clear: mistakes do far more to help us learn and improve than successes. As examples from both science and everyday experience can attest, if we treat each mistake not as a misstep but as a learning experience the possibilities for self-improvement are limitless.

Taken together, then, the overall structure of a five paragraph essay should look something like this:

Introduction Paragraph

- An attention-grabbing "hook"
- A thesis statement
- A preview of the three subtopics you will discuss in the body paragraphs.

First Body Paragraph

- Topic sentence which states the first subtopic and opens with a transition
- Supporting details or examples

- An explanation of how this example proves your thesis

Second Body Paragraph

- Topic sentence which states the second subtopic and opens with a transition
- Supporting details or examples
- An explanation of how this example proves your thesis

Third Body Paragraph

- Topic sentence which states the third subtopic and opens with a transition
- Supporting details or examples
- An explanation of how this example proves your thesis

Concluding Paragraph

- Concluding Transition, Reverse "hook," and restatement of thesis.
- Rephrasing main topic and subtopics.
- Global statement or call to action.

More tips to make your essay shine
Planning Pays
Although it may seem like a waste of time – especially during exams where time is tight – it is almost always better to brainstorm a bit before beginning your essay. This should enable you to find the best supporting ideas – rather than simply the first ones that come to mind – and position them in your essay accordingly.

Your best supporting idea – the one that most strongly makes your case and, simultaneously, about which you have the most knowledge – should go first. Even the best-written essays can fail because of ineffectively placed arguments.
Aim for Variety

Sentences and vocabulary of varying complexity are one of the hallmarks of effective writing. When you are writing, try to avoid using the same words and phrases over and over again. You don't have to be a walking thesaurus but a little variance can make the same idea sparkle.

If you are asked about "money," you could try "wealth" or "riches." At the same time, avoid beginning sentences the dull pattern of "subject + verb + direct object." Although examples of this are harder to give, consider our writing throughout this article as one big example of sentence structure variety.

Practice! Practice! Practice!

In the end, though, remember that good writing does not happen by accident. Although we have endeavoured to explain everything that goes into effective essay writing in as clear and concise a way as possible, it is much easier in theory than it is in practice.

As a result, we recommend that you practice writing sample essays on various topics. Even if they are not masterpieces at first, a bit of regular practice will soon change that – and make you better prepared when it comes to the real thing.

II

Should Plastic be Banned

Plastic bags are a major cause of environmental pollution. Plastic as a substance is non-biodegradable and thus plastic bags remain in the environment for hundreds of years polluting it immensely. It has become very essential to ban plastic bags before they ruin our planet completely. Many countries around the globe have either put a ban on the plastic bag or Levi tax on it. However, the problem hasn't been solved completely because the implementation of these measures hasn't been as successful.

Problems Caused by Plastic Bags

Here are some of the problems caused by plastic bags:

Non-Biodegradable

Plastic bags are non-biodegradable. Thus, disposing of the plastics is the biggest challenge. T

Deterioration of Environment

They are destroying nature due to their harmful effect. Plastic bags have become the main cause of land pollution today. The plastic bags entering into the water bodies are a major cause of water pollution. Hence we can conclude that these are deteriorating our environment in every possible way.

Harmful for Animals and Marine Creatures

Animals and marine creatures unknowingly consume plastic particles along with their food. Research shows that waste plastic bags have been a major reason for untimely animal deaths.

Cause of Illness in Humans

The production of plastic bags releases toxic chemicals. These are the main cause of serious illness. The polluted environment is a major reason for various diseases which are spreading easily in human beings.

Clogged Sewage

Waste plastic bags are the main reason for trapping the drains and sewers, especially during rains. This can result in a flood-like situation and disrupt the normal life of people.

Reasons to Ban Plastic Bags

There are numerous reasons why the government of various countries has come up with strict measures to limit the use of plastic bags. Some of these include:

- Waste plastic bags are polluting the land and water immensely.
- Plastic bags have become a threat to the life of animals living on earth as well as in water.
- Chemicals released by waste plastic bags enter the soil and make it infertile.
- Plastic bags are having a negative impact on human health.
- Plastic bags lead to the drainage problem.

Public Support for Plastic Bag Ban

Although the Indian government has imposed a ban on the usage of plastic bags in many states. But people are still carrying these bags. Shopkeepers stop providing plastic bags for few days only in the beginning.

It is time when we all must contribute our bit to make this ban a success. Thus we the educated lot of society must take it as our responsibility to stop using plastic bags. In this way, we can support the government in this campaign.

Some contributions that can be made by people are as follows:

Keep a Tab

In order to be successful in this mission, we must keep reminding ourselves about the harmful effects of the plastic bags on our nature and keep a tab on their use. Gradually, we will become habitual to doing without these bags.

Seek Alternatives

There are many eco-friendly alternatives to plastic bags like reusable jute or cloth bag.

Reuse

We must reuse the plastic bags we already have at home as many times as we can before throwing them away.

Spread Awareness

While the government is spreading awareness about the harmful effects of plastic bags, we can also spread awareness through word of mouth.

Conclusion

Although plastic is becoming a big threat for all of us, still this problem has often been overlooked and underestimated. This is because people do not look at the long term effect of these small, easy to carry bags they use in their everyday life. Besides all of these people keep using bags due to their convenience. But now everyone has to completely stop using the plastic bag to save our environment and earth.

III
Rising Prices

Rising prices break the backbone of common man. In India, price rise is a regular feature. Sometimes the government raises the prices. Sometimes thing go underground. People have to buy them in the

black market.

They have to pay higher prices. The government of India tries to check it. But it has not yet succeeded. So common people are hard hit.

There are many causes for price rise. Sometimes the production of thing goes down of it may not be as much as people demand them. If the supply is short, the demand may be great. Naturally, prices will go up. In a developing country like India, we have to face such a situation.

Sometimes price rise is a must. If the price of material is high, the production cost will also be high. But on many occasions people have to suffer on account of the faulty distribution system. The artificial shortage of thing is created. Thus people are exploited.

Another cause for price rise is the fast a growing population. Our production does not rise at the same rate. So there is a real gap between the demand and the supply of things. The standard of living of even a common man has risen. Sometimes the shortage is real. Naturally there will be price rise.

But rising price have to be checked. The government and the public must try to raise production. They must try for a fair distribution of things. Black marketers and

holders should be severely punished. We may have more and more fair price shops. Every effort should also be made for checking population growth.

Though the government has done a lot to check the rise in prices, the problem has proved too much for it. Rising prices are at the root of many kinds of evils in society. So checking the rise in prices is the need of hour.

Indian can broadly be divided into three classes. On the top, there are rich. They are the people who have got everything in plenty. At the bottom there are the poor. They are ill - fed and ill – clad. It is seldom that they have their own house to live in. In between these two classes, we have middle class. The people belonging to this classare neither very rich nor very poor. They have to maintain themselves outwardly in a fitting and decent manner.

The middle class has gone from bad to worse since independence. Mostly, the people of this class are servicemen. They get a fixed pay. But prices have been higher and higher. Taxes have been increased manifold. It has become almost impossible for the middle class to make both ends meets. The process of even coarse grains, pulses and clothes have shot up. The middle class starves.

The middle is a class of mental workers. To maintain their health and efficiency of mental workers balanced and nourishing food is required. They must get milk and fruits. But the price of milk has shot up more than twenty – eight rupees a liter. Fruits are so costly that only the rich can buy them. So the middle class is unable to get the nourishment it needs. It is losing its health and efficiency. It is also expected to give its children good education. But the high cost of living has made all this impossible for the middle class people. If the present trend continues. This class will no longer be able to maintain its position and status. Unemployment has also adversely affected this class. In fact it is on the verge of extinction.

The dissatisfaction of the middle class people is dangerous for society. Mostly the people of this group are educated. They understand reality. History tells us that they have always have been the makers of revolution. Further, they being the custodians of custom and traditions of a country. Their place in society is very important. So the miserable conditions of this class is harmful for the nation.

The condition of the middle class must be improved. Articles of daily necessity and ordinary comforts should be made cheap. The government should give it facilities of free medical and free education. The burden of taxes on this class should be lightened. Salaried people should be provided with the necessities of life at cheap rates. These suggestions if implemented can bring much relief to the suffering middle class family of people. Rapid social change make it difficult for people to adjust themselves to the changed order. This causes great suffering to this class. So change should be brought about gradually. This will help them in adjusting themselves. In any case, they should be helped to live well.

IV
Information Technology

Science has made great progress. New developments and inventions have been made. The world of Television, Telecommunication, Computers, the internet and all other audio – visual media is facing rapid and radical changes presently. Information Technology means the use of computers for storing, analyzing and distributing information. This is popularly known as IT. It has brought about a great revolutions in India. Miraculous development has been made in all field of human activity. In our present age, IT is playing the same role as roads and railways did in the industrial age. Computers have come to be used on a very large scale. And they don't work in an isolated manner. They have become inter – connected through what is called Internet. Information can easily be shared between friends, offices, shops, factories, banks, schools, libraries and so on. Through Internet one can easily have the information of far off areas without any delay and problem. One can chat with others through Internet. One can have the knowledge about jobs, courses etc. through Internet.

So, the Computer is the major segment of Information Technology which has spread in every sphere of existence of human society and has become indispensable. The present day accuracy, sophistication, efficiency etc. could not have been made possible without the invention of computers. Computer software are gradually becoming a decisive force in making important decisions. It has become the basis of modern scientific and technological inventions and researches. The use of software has been permitted in every walk of life, be it transportation, medical care, telecommunication, defence, industrial progressing, entertainment, office utilities space research, environmental predictions and so on.

Essay on Information Technology

We can classify the Information Technology into two major components.

Example:-

1. Hardware
2. Software

Hardware means the physical parts, which can be touched and are used to run the software.

Software are the programme or we can say these are the heart and soul of the hardware.

There have been tremendous ups and down in the IT industry during the last two decades. Information Technology has played an important role in making the Indian economy run at a much faster pace. During 2001- 2002, when there was worldwide economic slump, yet the IT sector managed to show an impressive growth. Though business volumes declined a lot, yet an awakening had been created among the youth and IT is must to go ahead in life. With IT becoming acceptable to all, it becomes apparent that people needed to know computers to excel in life.

According to the some recent studies our country will require millions of IT professionals in the next few years. It is expected that the demand of IT professionals during the present period will be much more than the expected availability. The emerging IT enabled service segment, has shown tremendous avenues of jobs for the qualified professionals. A study conducted by NASSCOM shows that this sector will create job opportunities for more than one million people

by the next few years. It is worthwhile to note that during the last 2o years, the IT industry's present trend reflects more than 20 times increase in the technical jobs sector. It is felt that with globalization, the opening of economic fronts and markets is becoming more competitive. Thus the demand of IT professionals will further increase.

After the attack on the World Trade Centre in America, the IT industry experienced some difficulties, though Indian IT field didn't feel the adverse effect as much as other developed countries. Although some Indian youth went jobless yet that was a temporary phase. The basic lesson that our country learnt after that incident is that "Our software industry has to be made more robust and less fragile, if we like to make it the most significant contributor to our economy." Tremendous market potential that is a available in our country is the area of television, education, telemedicine, entertainment, e – government etc., which needs to be given business.

Essay on Information Technology

At present our IT industry has provided job to approximately seven lakh people and earning only 15 billion dollars, which is less than one percent of the world market. At the same time a typical international software company with only 50000 employees, earns 20 million dollars through its worldwide operations. Based on the current trend, we will have to multiply our work force eight times. Today our IT industry is proud that 260 out of the fortune 500 companies are its clients. But these Indian software professionals are earning for foreign companies .If they are given proper opportunities in our country itself, then the things might improve and our own country would benefited.

Information Technology can contribute tremendously in the economic development, particularly the rural areas. It can become a prudent tool in integrating the nation, the remote localities that have so far been feeling a sense of neglect, will be feeling part of development. If we make computer education compulsory from primary and middle level, we can hope and aspire that within next few years, India will become a giant in the field of Information Technology.

V

Environmental Pollution

The problem of pollution has become very serious in recent years. The people of the developed nations try to solve this problem. But in India we have not paid sufficient attention to it. Our future generation will suffer from the harmful effect of pollution if we do not tackle the problem now.

There are different forms of pollution, such as water pollution, food pollution and noise pollution. Pollution of all these kinds result from the greed of men for getting more and more money. Trees have been cut down on a large scale.

A number of industries have been set up in almost every region of the country. So unbalanced industrial growth is the main cause of air and water pollution. The owners of the industries dump waste material on the surface of the earth or rivers, so water is polluted. The waste on the earth produces different poisonous gases which polluted the air. Forests which purify air have been cut down and new cities and industries have been established in their place.

Besides water and air pollution, we also face the problem of noise pollution. Today vehicles produce noises which are generally deafening. They cause tension, raise blood pressure and lead to several mental disorders. Food pollution is another problem that we have to face today. We suffer from several diseases by the polluted food item that we take everyday.

There are several causes of pollution. Today we cut down trees and plants. Trees and plants turn Carbon-di-Oxide into Oxygen. The air is not purified in the absence of trees and plants.

When forests are cut down we face the problem of soil erosion too. Artificial fertilizers are used to maintain the productivity of soil. We use polluted water in the plants and vegetable.So our vegetable and crops get polluted. Pesticides are also source of pollution of our crops, vegetables and fruits. There are more and more vehicles on our roads. They produce noises which are harmful for health.

The pollution of air and water will affect our health badly. We may not get breathable air. So, our health will suffer. We shall suffer from various diseases. In the absence of a fresh air, our food will also get polluted. If increasing pollution is not checked, we can not live a healthy life. Thus the very existence of life on earth will be in danger.

We must have balanced and planned industrial growth. In order to check this pollution, towns and cities should be planned carefully. We must not dump industrial wastes on earth or in the rivers. It should be destroyed by use of suitable chemicals. We should plant more and more trees and the cutting down of forests should be stopped. We should not use polluted water for imitation. Vehicles must use some new techniques so that they may not produce deafening voice.

At the sometime, we must continue our careful vigil so that we may live free from polluted air, water and food. Poverty leads to rise in population that stops all types of planning. A leakage in the nuclear plant at Chernobye in Russia affected the environment of whole Europe and some parts of the Asia too. Similarly population explosion in the regions having two third of the population of the world affects those areas too where population has been controlled. Poor people think that to meet the domestic and economic needs they should have morechildren. Every child in the family as soon as he is five or six years of age, starts earning. Although the earning of the child labour is quite meagre, the family partly rests its hope on him. In rural areas more population means more pressure on land, over exploitation of soil, over grazing and cutting of trees. This leads to environmental problems. More water is consumed by the increasing population. Cutting of trees means lesser rains. It leads to the compulsion of fetching of drinking water from distant places. It requires more children.

Rising in population means fragmentation of land. Scarcity of water means soil erosion. Increasing population requires more firewood. It again leads to cutting of trees and consumption of weeds. It means either scarcity of water or sometimes floods leading to wastage of fertilizers. Thus poverty leads to rise in population. Rise in population leads to conditions that spoil the environment. Environmental pollution affects human health that again leads to poverty. The vicious circle goes on.

With the rise in the number of family members, migration is the only way to secure employment. The migrated people live in slums where again there are problems of water supply, situation concentration of industrial waste and city garbage. The small treatments inhabited by slum dewellers become centres of immoral sex activities leading again unproportionate rise in population. A city like Mumbai has hundreds of slums that pollute the environment of the whole city.

The UNICEF report for the last decade of the last century gave a warning that if poverty, rapid population growth and environmental decline are not controlled, then there will be

increase in social division, economic disruption and political unrest. The fear is that the problem faced by the poorest people with poorest countries will continue to occupy a lowly place on the international agenda.

The UNICEF report also indicates that 29% of the population in Urban India and 33% in rural areas continues to live below the absolute poverty level. Pakistan share on health is only 1%.

The air is polluted by the smokers both in rural and urban areas. Efforts have been made by the government and non – government organizations to stop this nuisance. But it has not been taken up as serious problem. People are seen smoking even in the air conditioned compartment.

VI
Internet

The internet has become very common these days. This is one of the greatest inventions of science. Everybody talks about the internet now - a - days, but most people don't really know, what actually it is. Briefly, speaking, "Internet is a web which has a very large number of computers connected to each other." These computers are connected with one and another either through wire, satellite, or microwaves. They are so programmed that one can communicate from one computer to another computer within seconds.

In other words, the Internet is essentially a big network that links smaller networks and individual computers all over the world using moderns, phone lines, and satellite links. In order to communicate information to travel on Internet, a computer breaks down the information/ message into smaller chunks of data called packets and sends them through a 'Modem', and through the telephone lines. The Internet works in such a wonderful manner that even if one or the other phone lines are busy or a number of the individual networks go down, the information will still reach the final destination.

The Internet contains different parts with the most famous being the World Wide Web(w.w.w). As the name suggests, the web is a kind of net of a vast number of lines that connect computers all over the world. Different organizations and people have their own websites which lie on the web. Through an Internet connection, we can have access to these sites. If you want any type of information, you can get it from the web. The web also gives users the ability to jump from site to site by simply clicking the highlighted sections of text, called Hyperlinks, that appear on most sites.

For example, if you're reading an online magazine's review of a current movie, you might come across the director's name highlighted in blue color within the body of the text. By clicking on it, you can get information about him Another important feature of the internet is Email(Electronic Mail) where you can send your letter, message, or document through the internet within seconds.

However, like every invention of science, the Internet too has its good and bad points. With the easy possibility of Internet access, the Internet is being misused not only by the youth and kids but also mature people. The easy availability of Pornography is causing havoc in society. In spite of laws and the rules to prevent the misuse of the Internet, no resultant action is taken, and that to a great extent responsible for the degeneration and disintegration of the youth of today. The increase in sex crimes, the moral degradation of youth, the increase in the cases of young bodies and girls involved in sexual relations, can be largely attributed to the Internet.

The Government, various organizations, and even the public are well aware of the fact, but find no solution to stop the misuse of the Internet. The Government has to tackle this situation in order to keep the youth away from pornographic sites on the Internet.

In conclusion, we see how the internet has changed and made our lives easy in various ways. the internet can be thought of as a massive ocean if used in the right way, it can be very productive and helpful.

FAQ's:-

Q.1 What is the Internet?

Answer: The Internet is a collection of computers connected by network cables or through satellite links. Rather than connecting every computer on the internet with every other computer, individual computers in an organization are normally connected in a local area network(LAN). One node on this local area network is physically connected to the internet. So the internet is a network of networks.

Q.2 What is the importance of the Internet?

Answer: The Internet is a part of our daily life. It provides information, resources, and a platform for interaction.

Q.3 How does the internet help in communicating?

Answer: We can now communicate with our loved ones using the internet. we can video call and connect with our relatives.

VII

Should Students get limited access to the Internet

The Internet is one of the prime needs of today's world. The Internet is where we can find information about everything under the sky. It is the most needed thing around the globe. Businessmen, teachers, traders, students, everyone is dependent on the internet for their work. No matter if you are a middle-class person or a millionaire, all you need is the internet, sometimes for your work and sometimes for entertainment.

If we talk about students, there are many uses of the internet in a student's life. e-tutorials, college projects, exam preparations any many more activities can be done on the internet which can help students in their studies. But the fact that excess of anything can be harmful is applicable here also. Here we will discuss why students should get limited access to the internet and talk about the harms associated with the overuse of the internet by the students.

Effects on their Mentality and Family Life

This is the most serious problem among the students today. They spend the maximum part of their day on the internet and hardly have any interactions with their family members. This leads to weak family bonds. The students who spend most of the time surfing the internet end up with an unhealthy body due to lack of physical exercise, low grades in academics because they just keep on surfing useless things, and a distance from family members because they don't have time to sit with family and talk.

Students ignore their health, wealth, social, and personal life. The only thing they bother about is being online. We can see the examples of students getting mentally and physically disturbed due to internet addiction, for example, in 2018, a girl from Vietnam was addicted to Facebook and ended up in a mental hospital. Now she is under treatment. Another case happened in Taiwan where a student died because he played an online game continuously for 2 days without eating anything. There are endless cases like this happening with students due to the excess of the internet which reminds us how important it is to limit the internet access for the students.

Adult Websites, Pornography

Students need to focus on their studies and not pay attention to useless and bad things. But on the internet, they can easily get introduced to porn websites. These kinds of websites are available in large numbers. There can be a chance that students can reach these sites accidentally and get addicted later. As students are not mature enough to understand everything, they can be a threat to the girls around them. The students who are introduced to pornography at an early age can commit crimes and rapes. There are many cases where we can see the evidence of these kinds of crimes by the school or college students just because they get addicted to these bad websites. The sexual predators are chasing young school boys and girls and pretend to have the same hobbies and finally lure them into the world of pornography. There are many cases of lost and exploited young students due to these predators. These crimes are another reason to limit Internet access for students.

Physical Harms

The overuse of the internet is physical harm for students. Students are the future of this world and they must stay healthy to focus on their studies and become responsible citizens on this earth. With the excess of the internet, we can see many students spending hours in front of their computer screens. They keep on playing online games and chatting on social sites. this leads to their back pain, muscle weakness, eye problem, and many other posture-related issues. All these physical issues directly affect their studies and make them lazy. The Internet is a web where students easily get addicted and make their life hell.

The Social Life is Effected

A student needs to have a social life, make friends, and have face-to-face interactions but due to the overuse of the internet, these interactions have lost somewhere. The Internet is famous for meeting new people and making new friends but they have nothing to do with the people around us. Students get addicted to messaging and virtual communications rather than going out and meeting friends. This affects their social life and they no longer find it comfortable to have face to face interactions. The students are lacking communication skills and going away from their relationships and all the blame is on the excess of the internet. If we observe, we can find endless such cases near us where students are risking their future. It is important to limit the internet access for the students to save their social life also.

Cheating

The students getting excess of the internet can lead to cheating. The fact that the internet has all the information can be used negatively by the students. They use search engines for finding the answers to their question during tests which lead to false results. Many schools have banned the use of mobile phones and the internet inside the school so that students can focus on their classes rather than surfing. This also enables students to achieve better grades with their hard work. The reduction in internet use can lead to awareness among students and prevent the cheating problem.

The cheating is not only about cheating in examinations but there are many cases where students are hacking the school websites and changing the grades and altering the student's information. They hack their school websites to know the assignments and find their answers. In 2017, there was a case where a former student hacked his alma mater and changed his grades. The student was arrested but this is the time to think about what leads to all this?

Fraud

Dangerous games like Blue Whale, Momo, etc are also part of the internet. They target students and young children to lure them to do useless tasks and kill themselves at the end. They do friendship with the students and after getting all the information and understanding their weaknesses, attack them emotionally, and blackmail them.

In the year 2017-18, there were countless cases where students committed suicide due to Blue Whale and Momo. These kinds of websites are a threat to today's youth. the students are more prone to exploitation and luring which makes the internet a very unsafe place for them.

Conclusion

There is nothing more important than saving the students from getting lured by frauds, cheats, and getting addicted to pornography. They need to have a normal physical and social life. Most importantly, students should focus on their studies rather than anything else. All this can be achieved only by reducing the internet access for the students. Although the internet is a very useful thing there are many harms also. It is better to allow students to use the internet for a limited time only so they do not get time for any useless online activity. The school is the best place for the students to learn, there is no need to search for every small thing to search on the internet. If we encourage students to search for books rather than the internet for everything, it can lead to a huge change.

VIII
Pollution Due to Urbanization

Long Essay on Pollution Due to Urbanization

Urbanization is a great concept which is required to develop any country. It refers to the concept of urbanising remote areas by building infrastructure which then brings about development. Infrastructure refers to all the buildings and institutions which are necessary for economic development to take place in an area. For example, educational institutions like schools, colleges, vocational learning centres are part of the infrastructure. Healthcare facilities such as hospitals and clinics, employment opportunities, food security, etc. are also part of the infrastructure of a country.

It is seen very often that a big corporation sets up shop in a rural area, and around this, infrastructure is built, and development and Urbanization take place. Jamshedpur is an example of such a place, where Tata Industries set up shop many years ago and made the area highly developed. Thus, Urbanization definitely encourages the people of a place to have a better life by giving them more opportunities to achieve good life through education, jobs, etc.

On the other hand, it must be duly noted that Urbanization is one of the leading causes of pollution in today's world. There are several different kinds of pollution, such as air pollution, water pollution, soil pollution and noise pollution. The facets of Urbanization contribute to each one of these types of pollution in one way or another. Factories and mines contribute to air pollution through the fumes that each of them emit into the air. The damage done to the water and soil around factories because of their flowing septic is harmful for both humans as well as aquatic life. Additionally, the noises that come from mines, the whirring of machinery in factories, etc. contribute to noise pollution.

Additionally, it is not only big industries which contribute to pollution due to Urbanization. Part of Urbanization is also the development of roads, which means more cars, buses, two-wheelers, three-wheelers, trucks, etc. on the road. These all contribute to noise pollution because of the incessant honking, and also to air pollution, because of the fumes that all motor vehicles emit. Even when we are stuck in traffic in an auto, it becomes difficult to breathe because of the fumes which surround us on the roads. If we are finding it difficult to breathe, imagine what so many fumes are doing to our planet.

Short Essay on Pollution Due to Urbanization

150 Words Paragraph On Pollution Due to Urbanization

Pollution takes place when air, water or soil becomes contaminated with unwanted substances. Air pollution takes place because of the fumes of factories and motor vehicles on the road. Soil and water pollution take place due to the septic waste being released into soil or water that surrounds a factory. Even oil spills are a major reason for water pollution, and all kinds of pollution can be very dangerous for living beings. Another type of pollution is noise pollution, which comes from the honking of cars, loud sounds in factories, passing of airplanes and trains, etc.

Urbanization is a result of the need to achieve economic development. It refers to when a relatively rural or remote area is made more urban by constructing roads, hospitals, schools, offices, etc. In this way, development is a result of Urbanization, which is extremely good for all countries.

However, all the great factors that Urbanization brings in, such as factories to work in, motor vehicles to drive, and so much more, all of these contribute to pollution more and more. Even though Urbanization is very important for a country, it is important to address all the kinds of pollution

Conclusion

Urbanization is a really great step forward for any country, and it is and should be the main aim of all countries. All people around the world should have access to proper healthcare, education, sanitation, nourishment and safety, and Urbanization is how we can help achieve this goal. However, in the process of meeting this goal, we cannot forget that pollution due to Urbanization does take place, and is very dangerous for the planet and, therefore, all species living on earth in the long run.

IX

Education Should be Free in India

Education is the basis of our successful future. Education should be free for everyone, because not every person can afford it. Nowadays, schools and universities fees are too high. Most of the parents, work hard to have an opportunity to give that education to their children. But, there are also a large number of people who cannot do it because their money is not enough for that. Children, who want to study, cannot afford that. Many families are faced with such a problem. Parents were very upset and deep in thought about what to do, how to find jobs with high salaries, and how not to disappoint a child. Furthermore, they needed money to pay not only university fees but also spent their earnings on tutors and extra classes that would help prepare for exams. Additionally, the transport expenses required money. Consequently, children had been left without education.

From an early age, they went to work, without any experience or knowledge. As you might have understood, they did not have any achievements. As a result, people need free education to be able to succeed. The government needs to make education free in India, to make the nature of education in India more homogenous and widespread.

Education is the right of every child, and not everyone is born into financially stable families. We can do our part, belonging to the post-modern era of civilized and educated individuals, by setting up private institutions where we can teach the slum children of our locality for free. These small steps can lead to bigger changes on a broader spectrum.

The Indian government should provide free education to support poor families and meanwhile, they should allow private firms to run educational institutions. The rich families who desire high-quality education can send their children to private firms. The government firms when competing with the private firms would result in delivering high quality in delivering their service.

Major Challenges faced by Education System in India

The major challenges faced by the education system in Indian are:

1. Expense on education
2. Expensive higher education:
3. Capacity utilization
4. Infrastructure facilities
5. Wastage of resources:
6. General education-oriented
7. Student-teacher ratio

Let's explain these points one by one below.

1. Expense on Education

A very big amount of funds should be allotted for the development of the education system in India. The lack of adequate funds is the main problem in the development of education. The expense for education in Five Year Plans has been decreasing. Due to lacking funds, most educational institutions lack infrastructure, and libraries, etc. Due to this reason, desired outcomes cannot be achieved.

2. Expensive Higher Education

University and professional education have become costly in India. The fee structure of professional institutes has quite a high charge. It is beyond the reach of the common man. The privatization of higher education has commenced the growth of profit-hungry entrepreneurs. Nowadays higher education is a much costly task.

3. Capacity Utilization

The world now needs creative minds and the Government must encourage schools to boost the students and utilize their capacities to the max and not let their ideas go unheard.

4. Infrastructure Facilities

Better infrastructure must be given mainly in Government schools. Since Government is now concentrating on digital education, they must undertake steps to provide all necessary facilities in the Government schools and rural areas as well

5. Wastage of Resources

Our education system is based on General Education. Most of the students leave school before completing their education. It commences to wastage of financial and human resources.

6. General Education-Oriented

The educational system is of General Education in nature. The development of technical education is quite unsatisfactory. So our education is unproductive. Therefore, the number of educated unemployed persons is increasing day by day. This has become a great concern for Government.

7. Student-Teacher Ratio

The number of students in search of proper education is way more in comparison to the teachers available. So, qualified teachers must be appointed to impart knowledge to the future of the country

Reasons Why Education Should be free in India

- Free education can help reduce existential nuclear, poverty, and climate threats.
- Due to the huge population in India, free education becomes a very difficult goal to achieve. Though, when medication is the right of the people and is given by governmental hospitals for free, the same should be done with educational institutions because basic education is the right of every citizen of the country.
- Since most of the country is not e-literate, due to booming technology and education going primarily online, has resulted in a large part of the population lagging way behind.
- To overcome the ignorance and blind orthodoxy among Indian people, education is very important and should be available to every single citizen, despite their financial stability.
- Free education would encourage more parents to get their children admitted into educational institutions, rather than making them work in factories and spoil their entire childhood.
- Most people in India, especially in the poorer sections of society, have more than two children. So paying for the education of all of them becomes very difficult for the earning members of the

family. Therefore, free education will be a convenient means of imparting education.

- Educational institutions must hire quality teachers even though education is imparted free of cost, otherwise, underprivileged children will only get wrong knowledge and information.
- Since more than half of the Indian population consists of poverty-stricken people and farmers, education should be free as most of these people cannot afford to pay for their children's education, and so they abstain from admitting their children into schools.

Conclusion

Government firms are not efficient as private firms. Private firms usually compete with each other and focus on delivering the highest quality possible to sustain their business in their competitive world. For these reasons, private firms deliver much better quality in their service than a government firm who is usually protected from the competition. Therefore, when we aim for the best quality education in our society it is required that education should be privatised.

Frequently Asked Questions

Q1. Is there any scheme in India to support the idea of free education?

- *Yes, the Right to Education Act has the provision of providing free elementary education to children of age from 6 to 14 years.*

Q2. How will the children get benefit if education will be free in India?

- Free education in India will bring a huge change in the lives of poor children. Very importantly, it will vanish child labor to a great extent and increase the literacy rate of the country.

Q3. What are the challenges India is facing in the field of education?

- There are many challenges in India regarding education like the education in India is getting more and more expensive. Middle-class or poor people find it hard to admit their children to schools and higher education. The infrastructure is not at all developed and the ratio of students and teachers is low.

X

Selling Tobacco should be banned

Nowadays millions of people are using tobacco around us and smoking cigarettes. These are still in the market due to the absence of strong rules and regulations. Tobacco is destroying the whole world slowly. It has a very adverse impact on the environment. There would be a 5% reduction in global deforestation because approx. 500,000 acres a year get destroy due to tobacco farming. Tobacco has been around for many years and it should be stopped but the economy cannot handle it. The tobacco reaching our children and non-smokers as well and destroy their life. Many organizations are working to convince people to stop smoking but it is really hard because people are already addicted. They accept the negative effects of tobacco and continue to smoke cigarettes.

The only people winning in the tobacco field are tobacco company owners because they make all the money. If profit falls all they have to do is advertise a little harder and profit will roll. The environmental tobacco smoke the second-hand cigarette smoke breathed by non-smokers is known as carcinogen and the most pollutant environmental pollutants many people die because of the second-hand smoke it causes many deaths like tobacco smokers to do there are many reasons for death from second-hand smoke "lung cancer is the best-known reason of second-hand smoke" the simple smoke is really very harmful then it really looks " when a person breaths in smoke a million particles enter in our body and the main material in the cigarettes is nicotine which affects our nervous system. Nicotine is a poison that is present in tobacco leaves that defends the plant against insect attacks.

Forms of Tobacco

- Cigarettes
- Cigar, little cigar, cigarillos
- Dissolvable products
- Electronic cigarettes
- Traditional smoker's tobacco products

Mechanism of Tobacco

Tobacco contains nicotine and it is an amine (it is a group of a compound which contain nitrogen) nicotine acts as receptors known as nicotine acetylcholine receptors which are present in the smoker's muscle and throughout the brain.

Nicotine helps to stimulate receptors to start a reaction that results in further release of neurotransmitter (chemical messages that move between nerves, muscle, or glands to affect many body function, mood, and behavior).

The nicotine receptor present in the brain is composed of 5 different units around the central nervous system. These units work in the way they respond to nicotine and affect the transfer of nicotine impulse so can each nerve produce a variety of responses to nicotine at different rates of concentration.

The low dose of nicotine can stimulate the central and peripheral system resulting in other effects like increases in heart rate in increase in a heart attack or blood pressure at high dose nicotine blocks veins, resulting in low blood pressure and changes in the body's capacity to releases adrenaline.

How can Nicotine delivered its effect?

Smokers can combustible tobacco products that contain more than 7000 chemicals. Nicotine is a very important component of tobacco. 100 components are added to tobacco to enhance its flavour and the absorption of nicotine

The cigarettes are a very efficient and highly engineered drug-delivery system. By inhaling tobacco smoke. The average smoker takes in 1-2 milligrams of nicotine per cigarette. When tobacco is smoked nicotine rapidly reaches peak level in the bloodstream and enters the brain.

Tobacco and Its Effect on Our Body Organs

1. Eyes
   a). Cataracts
   b). Blindness excessive tearing
   c). Blinking
2. Hair
   a). Odour
   b). Discoloration
3. Ears
   a). Hearing loss
   b). Ear infection
4. Brain and Psyche
   a). Stroke
   b). Addiction and withdrawal
   c). Altered brain chemistry
   d). Anxiety about the tobaccos health effect
5. Nose
   a). Cancer of Nasal Cavity, and Paranasal issues
   b). Chronic Rhinosinusitis
   c). Impaired sense of smell
6. Mouth and throat
   a). Cancer of lips, mouth and throat larynx, and pharynx
   b). Sore throat
   c). Impaired sense of taste
   d). Bad breathe

7. Lungs
   a). Bronchus, lungs, and tracheal cancer
   b). Chronic obstructive pulmonary diseases
   c). Chronic bronchitis
   d). Respiratory infection
   e). Shortness of breath, asthma
   d). Chronic cough, excessive sputum production
8. Heart
   a). Coronary thrombosis (heart attack)
   b). Atherosclerosis (damage and occlusion of coronary vasculature)
9. Chest and abdomen
   a). Oesophageal cancer
   b). Gastric, colon, and pancreatic cancer
   c). Abdominal aortic aneurysm
   d). Peptic ulcer (esophagus, stomach, the upper portion of the small intestine) Possible increased risk of breast cancer
10. Skin
   a). Psoriasis
   b). Loss of skin tone, wrinkling
   c). Premature aging
11. Urinary system
   a). Bladder kidney, and Ureteral cancer
12. Hands
   a). Peripheral vascular diseases
   b). Poor circulation (cold fingers)
13. Immune system
   a). Impaired resistance to infection
   b). Possible increased risk of allergic diseases
14. Others
   a). Diabetes
   b). And sudden death
15. Legs and feet
   a). Vascular diseases
   b). Cold feet, leg pain, and gangrenes

Why tobacco should be banned?

Check below the points of why tobacco should be banned:

1. Healthcare

Tobacco smokes contain more than 400 chemicals in it and out of these chemicals 250 are very harmful to the body and other are carcinogen and the other form chewable form contains 28 proven carcinogen has many of 60 % of cancer cases worldwide among men and 25% of cancer in women are tobacco included. People can be mainly vulnerable to the bad effects of tobacco. So that the ban on tobacco will help to reduce health issues.

2. Diminish tobacco consumption

The benefits of stopping tobacco are evident. This will be good for their health and their finances. Tobacco has become very expensive in many countries. Tobacco users also claim that banning tobacco may help them with quitting.

3. The fewer financial cost of society

In the united state, more than $ 156 billion a year of productivity is lost due to death from tobacco and diseases caused by second-hand smoke. Another $ 170 billion go to direct medical costs for smokers. If tobacco vanished, so would those cost to society researchers estimate that the 1964 surgeon general's report and the tobacco control efforts that followed it have saved approx. 8 million lives in the U.S. Tobacco causes over 7 million deaths per year and kill 1 billion this century if current trends continue.

Lungs and head and neck cancers which are most common in developing countries are included by tobacco in 80 % of the cases.

How to Control Addiction to Tobacco?

Tobacco is one of the most important causes of premature deaths in the world more than 6 million people were dying because of consumption of tobacco smoking tobacco causes exposure to a mixture of more than 7000 toxic chemicals including 70 known carcinogens which can damage our body parts it is very dangerous to the pregnant lady who smokes give births to an infant at higher risk of congenital disorder like cancer, lung diseases, and sudden death. Newly-identified risk of smoking is renal failure, intestinal ischemia, and hypertensive heart diseases

The risk of death is increased with the increases in the number of smoked cigarettes but like long the smokers lose at least 10-12 years of their life because of tobacco. Combustible tobacco use is extremely hazardous to human health and is responsible for more than 90 % of tobacco death and disease. The efforts by the tobacco industry to market safer–sounding alternatives such as low-tare cigarettes and water pipes so a top priority to avoid combustible tobacco products and the only way for an individual to eliminate tobacco-related harm full is not to use them.

Conclusion

Tobacco should be totally banned because of its severe health risks. To stop this habit, the government are working on the different solution the tobacco ban is a very complex issue the tobacco is known as a killer of humans for many years it occurs diseases like cancer, HIV, and other different diseases the world is trying our best to fight these types of diseases.

Frequently Asked Questions

Q1. What are the different forms in which tobacco is available in the market?

- Tobacco is sold in many forms like Cigarettes, Cigar, little cigar, cigarillos, Dissolvable products, Electronic cigarettes, Traditional smoker's tobacco products, etc.

Q2. What are the health hazards of using Tobacco?

- Tobacco is very hazardous for the human body. It can cause dangerous diseases like cancer. It affects differently on various body parts for example like blindness, High BP, Bronchitis, etc.

Q3. I am 25 years old and a regular smoker but I don't have any symptoms of cancer or any disease. Does this mean tobacco is not harming me?

- Don't think Tobacco is not harming you. It's a silent killer. You are just 25 years old. Maybe you are a new smoker and your immune system is strong that's why you are feeling any health issues but remember once you get older and your immune system drops, you will catch severe diseases. It's better to quit now and lead a healthy life.

Q4. I use flavoured Hookah once a week. It contains only 0.5% tobacco. Is it also harmful?

- Yes, It is harmful. You are taking it in a small amount, it will harm you slowly but remember you are playing with your health. Better to stop it now.

Q5. I have heard that cigarettes harm all the family members even those who are not smoking. It is true?

- Yes, It is true. The smoke from cigarettes harms other people around the smoker too.

www.ingramcontent.com/pod-product-compliance
Lightning Source LLC
Chambersburg PA
CBHW071311130726
47997CB00007B/2504